Billy Neal Moore

I Shall Not Die

Seventy-two Hours on Death Watch

Billy Neal Moore

authorHOUSE™

1663 LIBERTY DRIVE, SUITE 200
BLOOMINGTON, INDIANA 47403
(800) 839-8640
WWW.AUTHORHOUSE.COM

First published by AuthorHouse 02/21/05

ISBN: 1-4208-3262-X (sc)

Library of Congress Control Number: 2005901101

Printed in the United States of America
Bloomington, Indiana

This book is printed on acid-free paper.

Table of Contents

Chapter One:
Deathwatch

I do not ever remember at any time in my childhood at Kent Street Elementary School in Columbus, Ohio raising my hand in any of the classrooms, saying that my life goals were to commit a murder and be on death row, waiting in a death-watch cell; ever mindful of 3 days, of 72 hours, of 4,320 minutes, of 259,200 seconds, slowly-but-speeding towards my last breath on this earth. Is this really happening to me? What happened to that little boy? I must be dreaming, because everything seems so foggy. All of my thoughts were lost in the madness that was swirling on around me. It was as if I were having an out-of-body experience, watching myself sitting in a deathwatch cell in the state of Georgia, hours before my execution...MY EXECUTION!

The realization of my execution being scheduled for May 24, 1984 brought my mind back to face the naked truth—this is real, and not a dream. As I began to look around the deathwatch cell, a very subtle fear began to paralyze my heart. This cell was different from those on death row; it was twice as large, and the dull egg white walls appeared to flow right out of the floor into the ceiling without seams, held together by a massive row of gray bars. These bars exhibited the force and power of the State of Georgia that said to me, "There is not any weakness in our pattern and we are here to hold you until your appointment with death."

Although the cell was empty, I could hear a voice calling out to me from the depths of the emptiness, overpowering my mind and filling my thoughts with these words: "I am the spirit of death which lives in this cell; I am the destroyer of life. I will subdue you, arrest your mind, and steal your desire to live." Being pulled into this world of hopelessness, spiraling down the path of death itself, the darkness had already begun to wrap itself around me. I could physically feel the grip of death; it was cold, unbearable pain running throughout my whole body. I heard these words screaming in my mind: "YOU'RE NEXT! YOU'RE NEXT! YOU'RE NEXT! THERE IS NO HOPE FOR YOU, BILLY MOORE... YOU ARE GUILTY!!! MURDERER!!! YOU ARE GUILTY!!! MURDERER!!!"

Noooo!!! erupted a much stronger voice that said, pull away from this embrace with death; engage your mind and every thought into all the detail around you. Frantically, I began searching the cell to find something that would help occupy my thoughts, not allowing my mind to run wild. Staring at the bed for the first time, I saw the steel plate coming out of the concrete wall on the left side of the cell; a solid edge about one inch in height traveled around the complete frame, which was about seven feet long, three feet wide, with six holes cut out of the solid sheet of metal that made the bed.

The mattress was rolled up and sitting on the end of the bed. This was a sign that this room hadn't been used since the last execution; however, it still had that strange smell of death. No matter how many times they tried to clean the cell, it still smelled like death. The mattress was off-white with thin blue pinstripes running from the top to the bottom, just like the one I had on death row.

Sticking out of the center of the rolled-up mattress were two gray wool army blankets, no pillow, no sheets. One foot from the bed was a toilet and sink combination made of stainless steel, and above that to the right was a piece of sheet metal screwed to the wall as a mirror. Though it was highly polished, just like everything concerning the deathwatch procedures, the mirror only distorted my reflection.

Being in this cell, now I could really understand why some have committed suicide, just gave up and let the state kill them. The thoughts about being electrocuted: 26,000 volts passing through their body. One minute later, another 26,000 volts would pass through their body again. Then the third phase drops to 20,000 volts, and if that doesn't completely steal the life out of a person, (and there have been executions which didn't kill the person), a doctor would check for any signs of life and if there was the faintest sign of life, the process started all over again until death was accomplished.

The whole procedure of my last minutes on earth, my last meal, my last visit, my last good-byes; then the ritual of having my leg and head shaved, as the doom squad gathers in front of my deathwatch cell, hoping that I would resist in the slightest way during my last walk to the chair. Then they could use their powerful collective force to bring me under their will and take me to the chair, strapping me down at the chest, arms, and legs. Then the warden would read the execution warrant and ask me if I had any last statements that I wanted to say before my death. Watching the witnesses watch me, as they strained to hear what I would say.

I could feel the anxiety building in my chest as I thought of these things (because I have seen this drill over and over in my mind and in dreams for years), because there isn't any word from the courts or my attorney, there wasn't any news on the television or the radio that was favorable to my case as the precious seconds ticked away. Silence… has become my worst enemy, because I am helpless, and powerless to stop what is about to happen to me. All of my thoughts are running around in circles and the facts are screaming loudly in my mind again, that no one has ever come this far into the deathwatch procedure, being guilty, and not been executed, but lived to tell others the story.

The fight continued, battling thoughts, not allowing them to overpower me as I looked up into the blue sky through the skylight that was in the cell, believing God would help me. Taking a deep breath, turning to look at the two tables just outside of my cell, and taking a mental note of things on each table. The first had two green logbooks, coffee, coffeepot, sugar, packets of tea, and on the other was an old radio, telephone, and some newspapers. On the wall to the right was the television on a stand.

I forced my thoughts to how all of this started. Just a few hours ago, it was a very beautiful day with the sun shining brightly, a clear blue sky; warmth streamed though my cell window. Today was our cellblock's outside yard privilege for three hours. My thoughts were, *would the officers let me go outside with the rest of the guys? Being that I had an execution date in three days.* Charles was taking up the list of names of those who wanted to go on the yard, and when he got to my cell, I added my name too. "Yeah! Place me on the list," not knowing if the officers would even consider me being on the list, and sure enough, my name was approved.

To physically get on the yard, there was a very long and intense process that each man had to endure once the captain approved the list. Everybody was locked down in their cells and the cell house officer would start at the top of the list after the extra group of security officers arrived to assist for security purposes. Then the officer in the office would start at the top of the list and unlock each cell one by one.

My door popped open and I proceeded out of my cell and down the stairs to the double cell doors; the officer would open one door and allow me to go into the cell, and through it into another cell. At the other door, the first door would be closed, then the officer would open the second door that led into a long hallway. After stepping into the hallway, the cell door was closed behind me. At the end of the hallway there was another officer waiting who was asking for all my clothing; everything, one piece at a time. Getting undressed in front of the officer was another form of how the prison routinely stripped me and others of the sense of being a human being. I handed him my T-shirt; he would look at it and feel around all the edges then drop it on the floor. Next the pants, the socks, the gym shorts, and last of all, my underpants; I was standing naked before this man (and sometimes a woman) and many of the other officers who were walking in the area, male or female. Any sense of decency that I had was carelessly dropped to the floor as my clothes were piled up just outside the gate.

The hardest part of the strip search was being told to turn around and lift up my feet so that he could see the bottom of them, then bending over and spreading my cheeks (my buttocks). Then I would have to open my mouth and stick out my tongue so the officer could see if there was anything in my mouth. This being completed, the gate was opened and I was told to get my clothes, and escorted to the gate that led outside, where I was allowed to get dressed and go out into the yard. The majority of the thirty-four inmates in G-4 cellblock would come out on a nice day like today.

Most of the inmates didn't want to be around me today because of fear; not knowing what was going to happen to me or what to say to me. They had lived with me for ten years, and the thought of my execution made them realize that their own execution date was drawing closer. Only the Christian brothers came out into the yard; all were members of my Bible study group. The first one to come out was my best friend Warren McCleskey. Warren and I spent most of our time together in the same cellblock. Floyd Hill was next to make it outside; he was a man of great compassion, and the oldest one in our group. Jerome Bowden appeared next; most people didn't understand him, because he stayed to himself. Once you got to know Jerome, he would talk to you. Jerome was the only black man I knew who liked hard rock music and could sing every song he heard. Charles Bowen came bounding outside, and as usual, he had his wonderful smile. Charles was our music director and he knew all the church songs and taught them to us. Fred Gilreath was very strong in the Lord and he was a man after God's own heart, who would teach the Bible study class some of the time. The last to file outside was Charles Corn; he was a very sensitive man that most people did not understand, and he was quick to say "Forget it, man," to avoid an argument.

Once we all were gathered on the yard, we prayed. I led the prayer. My prayer was for my Christian brothers for their strength during these last few days. That regardless what happened to me, they would continue the classes and go forth on their own. I had been their teacher, but I wanted these men to know that they belonged to God. The Lord was more than able to bring them through, as long as they keep the faith until the end. As Christians, I taught them to believe their life was theirs. As St. Paul said "to die is to gain and to be immediately in the presence of the Lord."

That alone was our hope in this situation, whether we were on the inside or outside of prison. While I was praying, the guards called out and said it was time for me to come inside because I was going to deathwatch, but I continued to pray and encourage my brothers. As I stopped praying, I looked into the faces of each man.

They all had tears in their eyes or running down their faces. I hugged each one and told them to trust in the Lord and that I would see them again. I told them that this was not the end and to cheer up and be strong. Just the sight of their hurt put a heavy burden on my soul, and I thought, *Lord, please help my brothers.*

Warren said, "Man, I know, but it's so hard after watching the others go and never return."

Jerome said, "It's been good, Moor-man. I'll see you on the other side." With that, he covered his face as he cried and walked away.

Charles Corn, being choked up, just walked away, shaking his head; he could not say anything.

Fred said, "God bless you, brother." That was all he said before tears rolled down his face.

Charlie Bowden, our choir director, said, "I can't say good-bye, but farewell. I love you, Moor-man."

Floyd Hill said, "Moore take care of yourself."

I went to each brother, hugging them and telling them that our God shall provide for me and that this battle is not mine, but the Lord's and He has never failed. After that, I turned and began to walk towards the officer who was waiting. I could hear and feel my heart pounding in my chest as the spirit of grief and sorrow began to bring each face, each word of my brothers clearly to my mind, and this flooded my own eyes with tears.

I approached the outer gate where the officer was standing. He said, "Moore, it's time for you to be taken to deathwatch. There is a buggy on the inside of the cellblock for your things; then you'll be called into the captain's office." With all of the emotions from

8

leaving the brothers, to the holding area just outside of the building, between the yard and the gate, there I began the degrading process of disrobing, but this time it was done outside. Nothing ever stopped the officers from doing the strip searches. Passing all of my clothes to the officer through the bars as he stood there watching me, I could see that there was something different in this search. The officer didn't conduct any conversation or smile. There appeared to be a lot of fear in the officer's eyes, as he used great detail to search my clothes, turning everything inside out and looking at all the seams, feeling them, bending them, looking for anything that could be a weapon.

My mind was racing out of control; thoughts were at war within me. This was a new and different direction in my life on death row. I could see fear in the officer's eyes—not that he was afraid of me, but the execution procedure that was now in progress. His not knowing how I would respond to my last hours of life... I could see this in his face. He opened the gate. I stepped into the area between all four cellblocks and I picked up my clothes and walked to the gate that led into G-4 cellblock. I saw the same fear in the eyes of all of the other officers as they were staring at me. Maybe all of them thought that I was going to go on a wild rampage, since in their mind, a man on death row has nothing to lose, especially so if he has an execution date like me. I noticed that all of the officers were in the alert mode, and had I made the wrong move, I would have been quickly put down.

After getting dressed, I retrieved the buggy and began to push it through the last set of gates into the cell area towards the stairs, struggling to pull it up the narrow steps. Some of the inmates began to shout, "You hang in there, Moor-man. Don't let them get you down, and keep your head up. I'm praying for you, man." Many guys came up to the front of their cells to get a last glimpse of me. My cell door was already open, but the buggy was wider than the door, so the officer told me to just go in my cell and lock the door and put my things through the bars into the buggy.

As I began to take my things out of the cabinet and place them into the buggy through the bars of my cell door, I began to recall how each item came into my possession. (As I picked up my Nikes, Sid and Melba Cook's faces flashed across my mind. I met Sid at Reidsville State Prison, where death row was in the beginning. Sid was allowed into the prison on death row with a group of ministers, yet he was the only one who wasn't a minister with a license, but licensed and commissioned by God. Sid is about six-foot-two, very soft-spoken, and wore glasses. He has the spirit of God flowing from him with such overwhelming power, that as we began to talk about the Lord, it was a real spiritual connection in the Lord.

Years later, when death row was moved to Jackson State Prison, I met Melba. She is truly a lady of God, one of the sweetest people, very compassionate and full of wisdom. As I was putting a sweatsuit into the buggy that was given to me by Pastor Fred Kelly of the Landmark Christian Church in Norcross, Georgia, Fred's face jumped into my mind's eye. He is a big man, big in the scene that his presence seems to fill the room because of love that flows forth freely from him. Then there is his beautiful voice: for preaching as well as singing. But most of all, he has unsurpassed compassion, and a love for others that flows right from his spirit. In his presence, I knew that I was with a man who heard from God daily and was able to share that truth with me.

I thought of many friends who had sent these things over the years, how we came to be friends, and all of the letters that we exchanged; sharing our problems and watching God solve them, and now they were worried about my welfare. Some were afraid, wondering how all of this would turn out. Would I be executed? With those thoughts, I began to pray for each person as they came into my mind's eye while I was packing. I was seeing a small series of mini-movies of each person, their faces and voices during our last visit together.

Before I could finish packing, the Christian brothers from the yard started to file into the cellblock and came up to my cell. But the cell house officer's voice came over the intercom, telling everybody to lock down in their cell because officers were coming into the cellblock to get me. Then he said, "Moore, are you finished?" I could hear the doors opening and the officers coming up the steps.

As two officers arrived at my cell, one of them said, "You know the drill." Which meant that I was to strip again and hand the officers my clothes through the cell bars. After they looked at them, they would return them to me, and I would put them on. However, a deadly silence fell in the cellblock. All of the inmates were straining to hear what the officers were doing. I can remember this quiet moment very well. As other men were taken to deathwatch, I too would be trying to hear what the officers were saying to them as they were packing. The only thing that all of this reminded me of was the movie, *The Ten Commandments,* the plague of darkness on the Egyptians. It was said in the movie that they could feel the darkness... I could feel the spirit of death taking over the cellblock, and more so around me, more than ever before in my life.

The voice of the officer brought me back to reality. He said, "Open cell 41."

At that point, all of the inmates started to shout and bang their cups on the bars, saying, "Moor-man, keep your head up and don't worry, you'll get a stay of execution from someplace." "You guards better leave him alone!" "Hey man, where your God is now?"

I proceeded out of my cell and downstairs with the officers carrying the buggy (an act of kindness that amazed me coming from them at a time like this). As I counted each step, I began to remember the exercise of running up and down these same steps daily. It was fourteen steps to the top and twenty-eight to complete the cycle. There were so many memories as I looked into the faces of the inmates I passed. They were sad, downcast, and melancholy. Searching for direct eye contact with each man, I began to realize, this is the whole reason why I am on death row, and that is to be executed. Now the time had come when of the all appeals seemed to have failed, and now it was time for the last walk from the only home I've had in the last eleven years.

I had always looked for something positive to come from the courts, but trusting in the world system was the very thing that God had been telling me not to do; rather, look to Him alone. All of the articles in the newspapers, on television and radio were negative. At least they were united—*Moore is guilty, he pled guilty, so why is the state waiting around? Let's get on with this execution.* The papers were correct, I did plead guilty because I was guilty, and nothing the State of Georgia could do to me could equal the terrible mental anguish and pain that I lived with daily about the fact that I committed this crime.

I rolled the buggy to the captain's office. He said, "Moore, sit down. Orders from Warden Zant and the attorney general's office came down this morning of your execution date for May 24, 1984 at 12:15 A.M." After saying that, he showed me a copy of the execution order. This didn't come as a surprise to me, because the first of the month, Judge Walter C. McMillgan had sent me a copy of the very same order. It was out of character for a judge to send a warrant for execution to the inmate. When I received that letter from the judge, it brought forth mixed emotions. On the one hand, it appeared that my life was over, all hope was lost; in my hands was my actual death sentence. Coldness seemed to surround me with each word that I read, and these words were really putting death into my spirit, mind, and soul. Numbness gripped my mind and I just could not focus or think. It was like being in court again and hearing the judge pronounce the sentence in open court, losing strength and having to sit down on my bed.

Secondly, there was a small ray of hope; in the letter that the judge sent, he said that he didn't want to set another execution date, but because of all the pressure he was getting from the attorney general's office, he didn't have any choice. However, he gave me the maximum amount of time before the execution could take place, which was twenty days. Why was this a ray of hope to me? Because this was the same judge who heard the case and thought that I would never be executed because he believed that the death penalty would not become constitutional in the state of Georgia and that I would just sit on death row for the rest of my life. Now that things didn't work out according to his plans, he was struggling with the execution of the death sentence, and that gave me some comfort.

The captain told me that there were some forms that I had to read and sign, acknowledging that I completely understood that I was to be executed. 1) I had to sign a form that would release my dead body to the prison or ship it back home to my family in Ohio at their own expense. I chose to have my body released to the prison. I felt that if the state took the time to kill me, then they should have the responsibility to bury me. I did not want my family to see me in this condition and then have to bear a financial burden. 2) Next, I was required to sign a form that stated how I wanted any monies in my prison account to be used. It could be sent home or be placed in the guard's fund. 3) The last was, who did I want to be my chaplain during my last minutes and to walk with me to the electric chair? My choice was Minister Murphy Davis, and that caused a big ruckus among the officers, because she was not one of their paid staff members. But Warden Zant allowed it grudgingly, because I said that I would have my attorneys file a lawsuit that would naturally cause the execution to be stop because my religious civil rights were being violated.

Going through these processes caused everything to become alive within my own mind, more than ever before. Now it appeared that this sentence was really in the process of being carried out. I watched the captain trying to be very professional about the whole situation. He had dark brown hair and dark brown eyes; he weighed 165 pounds and was five-foot-ten. He didn't smile much, nor did he make small talk with any of the inmates that I knew of. Nevertheless, he was a fair man. He was a "by the book" man, and you knew he would support the rules to the very end. He allowed me to take my Bible and address book, which doubled as my prayer list of all my friends. I was a bit surprised that I got to keep these items to take with me. Once I completed all the forms, the next issue was my personal items in the buggy. What was to be done with them? Should I send these things home or have the state dispose of them? I said to send the Bible study books to Christ Temple Church, Rome, Georgia and the other things to my son, Billy Jr. in Columbus, Ohio. The legal books I would leave for the inmates.

The last procedure was the removal of all my clothing while I was in the captain's office. One of the officers handed me a brand new uniform. I would be executed in this uniform. This seemed strange to me, because I wasn't given any underclothes or a belt, but a new pair of boots without the laces. I was told that this was the clothing I would wear for the next seventy-two hours. That statement propelled me into a time warp. Everything around me began to move in slow motion;

even the voices sounded slower! Time itself took on a new perspective. I could hear and feel every second ticking from the eternal time clock within my mind. The real countdown had started. However, I could feel the presence of the Lord as never before, comforting me through each step of the way. There was a special anointing on me like nothing I had ever experienced in the eleven years I had been on death row. My body was chilled because I had been fasting for the last four days, but now a warmth and peace began to flood over my body in a way beyond words or expression. I was safe in the midst of the storm! The PRINCE OF PEACE had surrounded me with peace, an invisible wall of protection, and I felt safe.

Chapter Two:
The First Day

Prior to this execution date, counselor Harry Nicholas would regularly call me into his office and we would discuss everything, even the possibility of my execution. He just was not my counselor, but a friend. He did believe in capital punishment, but not in my case, which led to many lively discussions. He was dealing with anguish and torment about my pending execution. He told me that he was going to write a letter to the Board of Pardons and Paroles on my behalf, telling them in his opinion why I should not be executed, saying that it was unfair for the Board of Pardons and Paroles not to consider the input of the counselors and officers who have personally spent time with me over the last ten years and knew me better than anyone else. I told Harry that this was not a good idea, since both of us knew the state's policy on employees getting involved in death penalty cases outside of their official duties.

Harry requested that Warden Zant allow him to write a letter on my behalf, but the warden adamantly forbade him, saying, "Do not get involved in this case." I also had told him that this was not a good idea and I would be all right. Yet, over my objections, he went to the Board of Pardons and Paroles.

Years later, he told me that upon his return to work from the board, two officers were waiting for him in his office. They told him that he was not allowed to enter his office, but was to report to the warden's office immediately. He was physically escorted—like he was an inmate—to the warden's office, and for two days, he had to sit outside of the office, just waiting. On the third day, Harry was told that there was another position open in another institution, and he should apply.

Everything was completed in the death row area with the captain and counselors. Two correctional officers arrived to take me to the deathwatch cell. I knew both of the them because they had worked on death row at one time, and their attitudes toward inmates were good. They treated the inmates with respect if they deserved it. Officer Cash was six-foot-two, strongly built, and possessed strong facial features. Yet he had compassionate brown eyes, neat short black hair, and a commanding voice. Officer Edge was stocky and solid, about five-foot-eight, curly brown hair, and he wore wire-rimmed glasses. My first impression of him was that he reminded me of the cowboys I read about in the Western books. He was rough and a quiet man; but when he spoke, it was with authority.

Both officers were the same rank, but it seemed that Officer Edge was in charge. He said, "Moore, it's time for us to take you to the deathwatch cell." Officer Cash produced a pair of leg irons, chains, and handcuffs. The chain went around my waist, through my belt loops. The handcuffs went through the chain onto my wrist, as the leg irons were clamped around my ankles. Very slowly, we began the walk down the hallway towards the gates that led to the regular population in F cellblock. As we came to the gate, the cell house officer at the gate gave me a sly grin that seemed to express his joy that I was going to be executed. Walking with leg irons was not easy and I definitely felt the pain of the irons cutting into my ankles. I wondered if I would ever come back into the area again to see death row, my old cell, other inmates, or my friends. It was not a bad feeling, but eerie and disturbing. (My first death walk and for sure my last; first time ever being this close to death and possibly the last.) Never before had things been like this for me on death row.

We passed through F-house, which is an open cellblock, meaning that there is one large building that is divided into two wings by a center hallway that makes four sides and an open passage. Each house holds 136 prisoners. On our way to the deathwatch cell, every cell in each cellblock was put on lockdown, allowing us to pass though without hindrance. Any inmate who was in the hallways as we passed was told to get on the wall, which meant for them to face the wall with their hands and feet spread apart as we passed, and not to turn around until we were out of sight. We only walked 150 feet that seemed to be 150 yards with those leg irons. We stopped at a red steel side door for the captain to come and pick us up, and then were transported by car to the deathwatch cell on the other side of the prison.

A white station wagon slowly arrived. The door opened and I could see the state seal for the Department of Corrections on the front door. The captain got out of the car, came around, and opened the door as the officers guided me into the back seat by holding my head, so that I would not hit the inside of the door. At least, that is what I thought from seeing this done on television.

As we drove, for the first time, I noticed that all of the doors on the outside of the prison were red. I'd been on death row for over eleven years, and never been on the outside of the prison to know anything about it. In less than five minutes, we stopped and the captain got out of the car and walked over to another red door as he was reaching into his pocket. Then I heard keys and the door open as the captain was looking around to see if there was anyone else in the area, waiting to try to stop them from getting me into the deathwatch cell. The coast was clear and the captain motioned for them to bring me into the deathwatch chamber.

Getting out of the back seat of a station wagon with leg irons and my arms handcuffed across my chest wasn't an easy task. I don't know which pain was worse—trying to move across the seat and get out of the car, or being pulled by the officers, which made the leg irons cut that much deeper into my legs. As we entered into the viewing chamber, my senses were attacked by a hospital smell, yet something was being covered up because there were two smells clashing together. (It was like when someone had put on two different types of perfume in one day.) I could faintly smell an underlying odor of burnt flesh—a smell I shall never forget. As a young boy, I had an experience of burning my hand, and you never forget that smell of burnt flesh, and here it was again. I could feel the struggle of death and life within my soul with each step I took in the house of death; coldness began to grip my body as if I had just stepped into a morgue. The feeling of death was overpowering and suffocating. Thoughts of dying were very strong in this room, and yet this place had the appearance of a chapel, where one would go to find life, though this was the house of death. There was a deep blood red carpet, three rows of pews on both sides of the room near the wall, and in the middle, there were five pews in each row. They appeared to be oak just like the ones in church.

At the end of the room in the center stood a red wall about ten feet wide with a glass window that was at least eight feet long and wide. Through it, I saw something covered by a white sheet. I have seen Georgia's electric chair before in books and on television, and in my mind, I knew that was it.

I was not prepared for what happened next! As we got closer to the chair, the officers guided me around the wall and right in front of the white sheet. With a quick move, he reached over, grabbing the sheet, and with one swift motion, pulled the sheet away. There it was... The Electric Chair; the instrument of death, the infamous Georgia Electric Chair. A dark, rich brown wood that looked to be very expensive, highly polished, and powerful! No amount of struggling would make that chair move one inch in any direction, as it sapped the very life out of the person who sat down in it, as the arms of death wrapped around them. (One thought screamed in my mind; it was as if I could hear the chair saying to me: *No one has ever sat down on me and then left the same way they came in, ALIVE!!! Look at the leather straps that will fasten across your chest, your arms, your legs. I will hold you until every ounce of life is drained out of your body.*)

I could see the cables leading from the chair and disappearing into the wall; the other end reached the top of the chair, snaking down to the bottom, connecting to the calf connection. A strong antiseptic smell lingered. They said to me, "Moore, this is where you will die in the next seventy-two hours, so you might as well get a good look at it now, because when you are being strapped down, you'll not be able to appreciate the beauty of seeing it then."

It happened so quickly that numbness ran throughout my body, as other thoughts began to surface in my mind, especially those from all of the books I had read about executions. Would the same things happen to me? Would I struggle against the leather straps as the current tore through my body? Would my skin catch on fire, and smoke rise from under the black mask over my face? Would I die with the first jolt or would it take more than that to kill me? All of these thoughts created instant fear. As I listened to these thoughts, I lost all the peace of God that I had earlier, and a fear bore down into my soul. Realizing that the spirit of death was establishing a stronghold in my soul, I found myself in a spiritual battle for my very soul right there in front of the electric chair. Moreover, I had to get my thoughts off this chair and dying, and focus on the Lord and regaining the peace that was with me while I was in the captain's office, or I would not make it the rest of this day.

I recalled scriptures into my mind from the Bible, how God is my shepherd, protector, shield, and life, and in Him, I move and have my being. My life is the Lord's and only He can take it; and only He can save me from this death. I had to confess that my life is spared [my not being executed] by faith as though it has already happened, and believe that no matter what I see with my eyes or hear with my ears, God is in control. Once I made that decision in my mind and refused to allow all those thoughts of death to have pre-eminence, the spirit of peace once again dropped into my soul, and my spiritual being from that point did not have any fear.

I was moved towards the deathwatch cell; as the door was opened, I stepped into the cell and turned around for the officers to take all of the leg irons and handcuffs off. They told me they didn't have the authority to remove them, and would have to wait until they heard from the lieutenant who was in the hallway, because the captain had left. After I was in the cell for about an hour or so, an officer brought me a food tray. This wasn't the last meal, just regular food: chicken livers, yellow rice, and cornbread. However, I could not eat if I wanted to because of my arms crossed across my chest in the handcuffs. I was fasting and had been for the last three days. My goal was to get closer to the Lord at a time like this, and not be distracted by everything going on around me.

I knew that my sisters wanted to visit, but I really did not want to see them, and my reasons were very selfish, because I felt that they would be upset and crying. I just could not handle that with everything else going on around this execution date. Therefore, I sent word through my attorneys that I did not want any visitors. But they never got the word, and I do not think that what I wanted would have mattered, because they came to visit the first thing in the morning, at 9:00. By then, the lieutenant had come through the deathwatch cell house and made the officers take the chains off. Then the phone rang, and it was a visit from my sisters, so the officers had me strip and dress in front of them. Then they put all of the chains on me again, but tighter this time. I believe this was done because the officers felt that I had gotten them in trouble with the lieutenant for not taking them off in the first place.

It was a long walk to the visiting room. As we would pass other inmates, the officers made them face the wall and spread eagle, as if they were being arrested as we passed. I heard them whisper to each other, "Is that the dude who's going to be executed Wednesday?" and others said, "He is the one. Man I'd sure hate to be in his shoes."

As we passed the visiting room, I was wondering where they were taking me. Turning the corner towards the outside of the prison, I saw my sisters for the first time; well, Norma had been there a few years ago, but I hadn't seem Regina since 1974. Making eye contact with them let me know that they were all right and that I did not have to worry about them. To my surprise, they were sitting there smiling, and that was a very

24

encouraging sign to me. A wonderful friend of mine, Ed Loring, was with them. We met in 1978 when I was on death row in Reidsville, the old state prison, during a visit, and we just hit it off. I should have known better than to think that the officer would remove the handcuffs and just lock all of us in the small visiting room by ourselves, no... the officer came also. My sisters hugged and kissed me. As everyone sat down, I introduced everyone to each other, since I was the only one who knew everybody. We tried to get comfortable and talk, but it was very strange with the officer sitting at the table listening to every word being said. But this was deathwatch, and we quickly forgot that the officer was there, and adjusted.

I asked my sister about my parents because I had received a copy of a newspaper clipping with their photo, and whoever did the story went to their home and wrote the story about them being the parents of William Moore, who was to be executed. I was told that the news of my execution was bigger news in Columbus, Ohio than here in Georgia. They wanted to know what my attorneys were doing in the courts and how at this point nothing was going well. The Georgia Supreme Court was on record saying that my case had been through their court three times and they didn't want to see it ever again.

Federal District Judge Edenfield also refused my appeal, saying that it was a second petition; therefore, he could not hear any of the issues in the case. The United States Supreme Court had denied our motion, so it looked very bleak in the legal system. The focus was on the Board of Pardons and Paroles. Everyone I knew was writing letters to the members of the board or making personal appearances. My trust at this time was not in the board, but in the Lord Jesus Christ. I knew that God's will for my life would be accomplished, and I was more than willing to accept it and go forward in the name of the Lord Jesus. That was all I had to depend on, as the apostle Paul said, "To live is Christ and to die is gain." I belong to the Lord and with that, I was at peace.

Strange as it sounds, during this visit, I began to learn more about my sisters. Since I was the youngest, I had no idea what either one of them was like until that day. Many people thought that they were twins because they dressed alike and had many of the same characteristics. They even bought the same clothes on the same day from the same store at different times. I knew that they were close, but not that close. Even now, they were finishing each other's sentences. They were surprised at the many people who were involved in my case from across the country. That was the working of the Lord, for thousands of people from all over the united States wrote letters. When Regina was at the parole board, she heard the employees amazed about all of the letters from around the country for this William Moore; who was he anyway?

I was amazed myself, because I purposely did not ask anyone to write letters or visit the board on my behalf. My thoughts were that all my help comes from the Lord, and if God did not help me, there was no help at all. Just knowing that, I really was at peace because I did not have to struggle, but rest in the ability of the Lord.

Ed Loring sat there listening very quietly, which was very unlike him, because he always had a lot to say. I remember the times at the state prison how he was teaching me theology; however, it was not the regular classroom type stuff, but Ed made it personal, and in doing so, the teaching made me a better person. Of course, some of it I understood and other parts went over my head, and yet it was fun to be learning, as he would bring the scriptures to life. Ed has a beautiful smile and a crazy laugh; he is truly down to earth in all of his relationships, and there isn't any falseness. What you see and hear is what you get from Ed. He filled me in on the operation of the Open Door Community that helps the homeless and death row inmates.

We stayed in the visitation room until 3:00 P.M., then the officer ended the visit. Everyone hugged me and said that they would be back tomorrow. Parting was not hard for me; my spirits were lifted, knowing that they were standing strong and my parents had hope. The officer and I waited for another officer to come and escort me back to the deathwatch cell, exiting the visiting room, waiting at the gate which led into the prison. A female officer made sure that there wasn't anyone in the hallway before she let us in through both set of gates. Heading toward C-house, the officer stopped at the mailroom to see if I had any mail. There were three letters.

By this time, I had been wearing the leg irons and handcuffs for over six hours, and I was in a lot of serious pain. Every time I moved, they would cut deeper into my flesh. We stopped at a red door just before the cell block as we entered. To my surprise, it led us outside

27

on the yard next to the deathwatch chamber. One of the officers opened the door and once again I was in the room used for viewing the execution.

Back in my cell, the painful cuffs were off. I rubbed the deep grooves in my wrists and ankles. I was looking for the officers to give me my letters, which were lying on the table. I asked them for the mail and was told that they had to call the warden to see if it was all right for me to have the letters. In less than five minutes, I had the mail and I was very excited. To this day, I can only remember who one of these letters was from. That was the letter from Evelyn, my mother-in-law. The words of her letter took my breath away. It was as if I was hit in the back of the head, nearly blacking out from the pain... She began by telling me that my ex-wife, her daughter, had written a letter for Evelyn to send to me during this time that I was on deathwatch, because she wanted to clear her own conscience and heart. As each word filtered into my eyes, the meaning brought the feeling of death just one step closer to my mind, as the images of the past began to fall into place. Things that really didn't make any sense to me for years now became crystal clear. The power of words, the unknown now became known; it was like knives being plunged into my heart as the truth began to pull all of the pieces of this puzzle together.

For years, fragments flashed on the screen of my mind with no connection or meaning. She said... Little Billy Jr. *WAS NOT MY SON*. Now that I was on deathwatch, why tell me now? Rage and hatred blasted through my mind, grabbing a stronghold on my emotions! It was a terrible fight; old thoughts surfaced of how she was the one who had introduced him to drugs when he was only fifteen years old. God had to work on my heart then, because I was so angry with her that if I could have physically put my hands on her, it would have taken the grace of God to keep me from hurting her. However, the Lord changed my heart about the anger that I had towards her, and I needed to be obedient to what God was leading me to do about the situation. I had to write her and ask her to forgive me for the thoughts of wanting to hurt her, and now this revelation.

I remember when we were teenagers and dating, both of us living in broken homes, wanting to make sure that our family stayed together; and our family would consist of three children. However, once Billy Jr. was born, at six weeks old, they came to Germany so that we could live as a family. I was in the army and stationed in Frankfurt. Then all of a sudden, she did not want any more children. Being very adamant about it, she took steps to make sure that she could not have any more children. Before she came over to Germany, and without telling me, she had the doctor put in an IUD shield so that she could not get pregnant. Both of my sisters would always say to me, "Little Billy will always be our nephew because you believe that he is your son, and if you love and accept him, so will we, but he isn't your son. He does not look like a Moore-baby; he does not have the small Moore-eyes. Look at his ears; nobody in our family has ears that are flat on the top like his does."

I would just dismiss their words, because I thought that my wife and sisters really did not get along at all, and that was the reason. Years later, as Billy would visit me, he would always have these questions, "Daddy, how come I do not look like you? Like anyone on your side of the family?" Then he would compare our hands, our ears, our eyes, and nose. I would ask him if my sisters had said anything to him, what was causing him to have all of these questions? (He would never tell me, but when he was living with his grandmother; His mother and her boyfriend Donald Green came over. Donald told Billy to do something that he did not want to do, and Billy said to his mother that Donald was not his father; why should he have to listen to him? She said that Donald was his real father.)

When he would say those things, I could faintly see images flickering in the back of my mind, but they would never come into focus. I would tell him that I thought he took after his mother's side of the family, and maybe her genes was stronger than mine, because he looked a lot like her. Other thoughts began to spring forth… She would always say that I was trying to take HER SON away from her, because he would always wanted me to hold him or come to me whenever he got hurt or wanted anything.

As I read Evelyn's letter, she said that her daughter's letter was confirming that Donald Green was Billy's father. Right then, all the pieces of the pictures came into focus; everything that had been scattered in the back of my mind was now clear, it was him! Every time I looked into Billy's face and saw those big eyes, ears that are flat along the top edge, and how his fingers are dark, especially on the nail, that is it, it has been Donald who I had been seeing!

It was like warp speed as thoughts began to overwhelm me; I would not be in this mess, about to die, neither would I have been under the tremendous pressure of trying to support a child who was not mine. I brought him to Fort Gordon to live with me because his mother was a drug addict, leaving Billy alone with anyone or by himself, not taking proper care of him. I tried to get the army to help me, but they said that it would take at least three months before I could get my own check restored and the extra money for housing because I was now living off the military post. Being that I was the parent with the child, it was the army's duty to pay me the extra funds for the trailer we had rented. Nevertheless, my greatest period of stupidity came when I willingly gave in to the pressure of not being able to provide for my son. (I am not saying that my ex-wife or the fact that I had Billy was the sole reason for committing this terrible, terrible crime.) The only thing that drove me to stay in the army as a career was the fact that I was a father and needed to provide for my family.

Not only was the state in the process of putting me to death, now the power of this revelation had taken over the position of stealing my life! Words cannot begin to express the depth of sorrow that flooded my heart that very second. My whole life was wrapped up in Billy; he was all I had to live for, and now that small glimmer of hope was violently ripped away; I could now relate in some degree to the tremendous pain that I had caused. This was like a death in the family. I felt defeated, dejected, and desecrated. The spirit of anger slowly crept throughout my body as every muscle began to tighten into knots. There was a scream building in the pit of my stomach, erupting like a volcano in my throat, choking all the air out of my lungs as if Mike Tyson had hit me in the stomach. There was not a sound falling from my lips as my body violently trembled, doubling over in pain as anguish caused rivers of sweat to gather in the middle of my forehead and creating a puddle of water on the floor. Electrocution now could not be worse than this news. I was completely losing it, my desire to live; and for what seemed like many hours of torment, the spirit of death had me again.

In the midst of struggle, I could sense the words... *IT WILL BE ALL RIGHT SON...stop thinking about yourself, your pain, your loss; do not even answer that letter, but minister to my people that I have placed in your path. This is the perfect time for you to realize this truth, that when you are weak, I AM strong!* At that point, it seemed to me that I was able to breathe again and fought to keep my mind on the people I was preparing to write.

After putting that letter down and reading the others, I asked the officers for pen and paper to write with, in order for me to answer these letters. He said that I should remember that I was on deathwatch and that I could not have anything in the cell.

It appeared to me that these officers were getting back at me for not allowing them to turn on the television or radio. The procedure on deathwatch was if I wanted either of them on, then the officers would have to turn them on, but if I did not, then they could not turn on anything. I was fasting and did not want to hear any of the news stations, so the officer had to just sit across from the cell and watch me, which was their job. Yet they did not like that at all. I sat on the bed trying to figure out what to do next, because I was not going to allow myself to be upset by this and drawn off my course of peace. One thing that has always helped me to be able to relax was to exercise, and with that thought, I pulled off my shoes and shirt and began to stretch on the floor. The officers really began to watch me. Neither said a word, but one started writing in the green logbook. First I started with push-ups, sit-ups, toe-touches, and I started to jog in place. All of this lasted about three hours, after which I was soaking wet with perspiration.

The night captain came in the deathwatch area. He at one time was the captain over death row and I knew him very well. When he asked me how I was doing, I told him that everything was fine except for one thing: I wasn't allowed to answer these letters that I had received today. He told the officers to give me some sheets of paper and a pencil to write with, and for that I was truly thankful and began on the letters.

The officers wanted to know how I could think about writing letters at a time like this. I told them it was a God-given gift, a special desire to help others, regardless of my situation; therefore, it was a privilege for me to write these letters. To me, this was the best from of expression and avenue of spreading the gospel of Jesus Christ.

After the completion of the letters, I gave them to the officer to mail for me, got out my prayer list, and opened my Bible and started to pray for all of my friends. In the background, I could hear the officers saying that it was too late for me to be doing that; I should have thought of that before I got into trouble. I just ignored them and kept on going down my prayer list of over 150 names, praying for each person according to the scriptures. As my prayers began to grow louder, I heard some other officers come into the cell block to see me, but I wouldn't stop praying and they said that they would come back later to see me. I knew that they understood because they had seen me in prayer many times before on death row. This was the Lord's time and my time with Him, and nothing was going to stop it. There wasn't time for me to see others while I was at the feet of the Lord.

After praying and getting up, I asked the officers to wake me up at 4:00 A.M., because I was going to sleep. I must have shocked them, because their mouths fell open and they asked, "How you can sleep at a time like this!" I told them that staying up all night would not change the fact that I had an execution date, nor would being up move any of the judges or the people on the parole board. Besides, none of that would be helpful for my own health, so wake me please. I do not recall any dreams, only that my sleep was peaceful. But at the normal time which I usually woke up, 3:00 A.M., my eyes just opened. I rolled out of bed to find two new officers. I asked them for toothpaste and a toothbrush and something to shave with, as I began to clean myself up for the day.

Getting my Bible, I sat on the floor and started to read and pray. I found over the years that the most effective way for me to pray was using the scriptures

34

and the Holy Spirit to lead me into prayer. I prayed for the people on my prayer list the first thing in the morning. Feeling the connection of my spirit to the Holy Spirit, I was ready to read the Word and allow the spirit to minister to me. I began to read psalms 51 and 147. I found it difficult to grasp what I was reading because of the other thoughts bombarding my mind.

Once again, I fought to anchor my thoughts on the Lord and not the things around me. There was a beckoning voice wanting to know why I was wasting my time praying when my life was on the line. I only had two days left, and where was my God now? Why would God make a difference between me and the other men who were executed? These thoughts began attacking me like a machine gun, and succeeded in distracting me. I stopped to take control over these thoughts and to bring them into subjection to the word of God that I knew, that God would keep my mind in perfect peace when I kept it focused on Him.

I turned the pages of the Bible until I came to Psalm 118, and was drawn to read it. This passage dealt with the love of God, which was really feeding my soul and comforting me with a fresh understanding. The life that is in the word of God just added more life to my spirit and brought the peace of God to me, that passes all human understanding.

As I read verse 17, which stated, "I shall not die, but live, and declare the works of the Lord," everything around me completely stopped! There was nothing but the presence of the Lord and myself—no officers, no deathwatch cell, no voices, a total place of calm and peace as the power of the Holy Spirit just rolled over me in waves of goodness that brought every word to life. In my mind, I could hear the voice of the Lord Himself actually saying this to me: "You shall not die in the electric chair but live and declare my works, the works of the Lord to the world." It was a divine implantation of God's word into my spirit and each word brought a freshness of life.

So much joy began to flow through me that I don't know how long all of this took place. I was lost in the midst of happiness; tears of joy flowed down my face and it was beyond anything I had ever experienced before. I was in a classroom with the Lord and He was teaching what He wanted me to know, not just a knowing of understanding something, but the God kind of KNOWING that transcends everything that was going on around me. I was not going to die in Georgia's electric chair!

It was amazing knowing that God had visited me in my time of trouble to bring forth His word of life in the midst of the state-planned death scheduled for me! This greatly humbled me as I wondered, who was I that God would even care or even be concerned with me with the thousands of men on death row in the United States? Moreover, knowing I was guilty of the crime! What a humbling experience in my life; what a confidence builder from the Lord! From that time, I knew the Lord had some special work for me to do in this life. I wondered just what this work of the Lord was. Could it be that I could continue the ministry among the inmates on death row that I had been doing for ten years? My thoughts moved toward a special work that the Lord had for me to accomplish in this life.

God wants people to know that he is not only a God of the Bible or the Old Testament, but also the God of the living right now. There is a blessing in serving the Lord now. How could I convince the men to believe me when I told them about giving their lives to the Lord and that not all hope is gone, even while on death row? By them seeing me alive would be the wonderful works of God. I would be a living testimony that God does work in the lives of people today. I am sure that all would recognize that the only way I was delivered was by the hand of God. I knew that I had to work for the Lord, and immediately I was once again aware of my surroundings and the voices of the officers in the background. I closed my Bible, got up, and walked to the bars. I spoke to the officers. "Good morning, officers. How are you today? Do you know that God just told me that I would not die but live and declare the works of the Lord."

One of the officers said, "That's all fine and dandy, but what have the courts or the Board of Pardons and Paroles said about your case? That's the only god you need to hear from right now." With that, he laughed and said, "Tell me, how is that going to happen? Is God going to come down here and open the cell doors and let you out? Will He file a petition in the courts for you?"

I replied, "I really don't have any idea or answer to how it will be accomplished. All I know is that it will happen just as God said! Keep your eyes open and watch the hand of the Lord. You will see it come to pass, and then you will know I told you before it came to happen." As I turned back to my bed, my mind was

37

full of excitement and questions. How is God going to do this? When would it happen, and where? This was almost too much for me to bear as the total excitement began to overwhelm me.

Chapter Three:
The Second Day

The case was in the Eleventh Circuit Court of Appeals and the last I had heard was that the three-judge panel refused to grant me a stay of execution. Even my attorneys thought all twelve justices would give this petition a second thought, because it was a guilty plea. Of course, there was the Board of Paroles and Pardons, but my thoughts were that the chairman would say I committed the crime, and to continue on with the scheduled execution date. I firmly concluded that this is work for the Lord alone. I would stand on His word regardless of what I see or hear. I turned to the scriptures again and re-read every verse like before. Every time I read those verses, I could hear that same voice ministering to my soul. From that point, I could not read anything else but Psalms 118:17-19. All my favorite verses seemed dead. It was strange, but it kept me focused in one direction and on one thought from the Lord. My emotions were running high, and I was full of energy. I was ready to tell my attorneys, who knew I believed in God.

It was breakfast time and my food was brought over by the cook. It was oatmeal with raisins, scrambled eggs, and two strips of bacon. I told the cook I did not want the food. He suggested I eat to keep my strength up, but I politely refused and thanked him. I did not need anything to distract me from the Lord and what He was leading me to do. The officer wrote something in the green logbook; probably that I refused the meal.

It was still early in the morning, around 6:00, and it was time for a shift change. Officers Edge and Cash had returned to deathwatch, which was strange to me, because I thought that I would have someone new every day. Our greetings were warm and friendly as always. One of them inquired if I had found out any good news at all. I was not watching television, listening to the radio, or reading the newspaper so I really did not know of any news from the outside world. I spoke up, "I can tell you this, hot off the press of God's reel. He has shown me just this morning that I shall not die but live and declare the works of the Lord. Moreover, that is all I need to know from God." Their expressions indicated that they did not believe me.

As I began to explain this to them, my heart, I was saying to myself, *Jesus I am truly convinced and settled that I will get a stay of execution. Even if no one else believes in your word, I don't care.* Reflecting on these hours was fearful, but I had a great peace within me, one that surpasses all understanding. I did not know what made me so special that God would spare my life and not the others who had died. I had served the Lord

40

for the last ten years on death row, and God had more work for me to accomplish. I was committed. I did not think that I was special. Compared to other Biblical figures who were common men and women, God spared them for His own reasons and then used them for His purpose to tell others how great God's mercy is, and to bring someone to the Lord. I just know what God has told me. As I shared this with the officers, I began to feel the warmth of God's presence. I knew this was part of His plan for me.

After talking to the officers, I wanted to call my mother and tell her, so I requested the phone. I knew my mother would understand, because she had multiple sclerosis for twenty-five years, and you would not even know she was sick, because she never complained. She was an encouragement to me to be strong in this place, and she was close to God. The officer dialed the number and gave me the phone. I heard my mother's voice: "Hello."

"Mama, how are you?" I inquired.

"Billy, is that you?" she asked.

"Yes, Mama, it's me and I'm doing fine. You know Norma Jean and Regina are here, and I should see them today in an hour or two. They seem to be doing good and not worrying. At least from their appearance, they were holding up pretty well." I was glad because it would not have been good for me to see them crying or falling apart. That would caused me to lose my focus, and direction; I need all my attention directed on comforting them. "Actually, Mama, when I first got this execution date and my attorneys told me that my sisters would come down to visit, I did not want to see

41

anyone. My thoughts were selfish, because that would make things harder on me to see them all disheartened. The attorneys told me it did not matter what I wanted because they were coming down to visit anyway. You know your daughters, once their mind is set on anything, they will do it. Norma Jean told me she felt peace about the whole situation and I was not to worry. Norma Jean and Regina have this ability to see a light from the Lord and said that I too should be able see this light, but I have not been able to see it or feel it. However, one thing I can tell you is that I got a word from the Lord this morning about this situation."

She was quiet for a few minutes and then asked, "What's going to happen?"

I replied, "God gave me these verses: *I SHALL NOT DIE BUT LIVE AND DECLARE THE WORKS OF THE LORD. HE HAS CHASTENED ME SORE BUT HAS NOT GIVEN ME OVER TO DEATH.* So I shall not die in the electric chair. I do not know how all this will work out. My attorneys are doing all they can and many others are helping. It is not my job to worry about how the Lord is going to deliver me, but just believe and watch God bring it to pass. So do not worry, it shall be all right." With that, I asked her to tell Dad that I love him and give him a kiss for me.

After hanging up the phone, I thought about what to do next until my 9:00 A.M. visit with my family. I got my Bible and began to read. Nothing I read was understandable. I knew what was being said, but my inward spirit wasn't touched at all. I thumbed through the pages and returned to Psalms 118:17, and once again it exploded in my spirit. This was the only

42

scripture I could read and hear God and be comforted within my spirit. I read it repeatedly, digging into each word, finding out just what each word meant. It was a wonderful time to sit back and meditate on the word of the Lord.

The phone rang and the officer informed me I had a visitor. Once again, I had to go through the leg irons and handcuff process. The officers had a brand new shiny, silver pair of leg irons waiting for me. One of the officers put the irons on too tight, not allowing room for the cuff to move freely on my ankles. Every time I took a step, the cuff would dig into the skin of my lower ankle. It was pain of the greatest magnitude; I cannot fully explain it for one to truly understand, unless they have experienced it. Quickly I learned how to shuffle flat-footed, sliding my feet on the floor. The chain had an individual handcuff extending from one part of the chain about six inches out on both sides. The officer had me turn around and face him as he slid the chain around my waist, putting the Master lock through the loops at the end. Then he slid the chain around until it locked in the back and the handcuffs were at my side. He moved my right arm across my body to the left handcuff and then my left arm to the right side, making an X shape across the front of my body. This is a most uncomfortable position, as you can imagine. However, I could not blame them; after all, this was deathwatch and my execution was looming large in their minds.

I thought that I had seen every exit and entrance into this area, but as we passed the shower, we turned left instead of right into a red door which was behind the shower. One of the officers pulled out a hand radio and informed someone that we were coming, and to clear the hallway. I could hear a key opening the door and we were between the cellblocks. I could see all the plumbing and into cells in G-house, which was the old death row cellblock. To my surprise, we stepped into the hallway just above F-cell house right before death row, and I could see the officers from where we stood. As we turned the corner, there were a few inmates in the hallway. The lead officer told them to assume the position on the wall. I am not sure if they understood him; knowing what that order meant was not in the prisoner's handbook, because they looked confused. The officer told them again and they quickly obeyed.

Here I was, a condemned man only hours away from my execution, and yet some of the treatment I received was like being the king or the president. However, I was neither, I was a dead man walking. We finally arrived at the visitation room. I wondered how my family would react to seeing me in all these chains. The door opened and Julie walked in. She was around five-foot-five, on the slender side, and had light hair, but what I recall the most about her, were her compassionate eyes and the terrific smile. Julie was working for my friend, Attorney Jack Boger of the NAACP legal defense fund.

At this point, she would be the person who would come to the prison and bring me the updates on what was happening in the courts, as well as papers for me to sign. I believe that she had just finished Harvard Law School and this was her first experience with the execution of a death penalty case. Therefore, they were not easy tasks. She gave me a big smile and asked how

I was doing. We hugged and held each other a little longer than usual. I told her that everything was all right, and this was the best treatment I had gotten since being in prison. We both laughed at that.

I told her to go ahead and tell me the bad news before my family visited. She said the courts had not looked favorably, since I had gotten the execution date. The appeal was with Judge Edenfield of the District Court in Savannah. She felt that he would be the one to grant me a stay of execution, since he had granted me a relief from the death sentence in 1980. She told me that Dan Givelber, my attorney, was the one who argued before Judge Edenfield, and that he was brilliant. She said that Jack was waiting in the Eleventh Circuit Court of Appeals in Atlanta if we needed to file the petition, and someone was in Washington D.C. to file an appeal with the U.S. Supreme Court. Back in those days, getting appeals around to the courts was nearly impossible, so people had to be stationed all over the area where the courts where.

Murphy Davis and Connie Rice had returned to Wrens, Georgia talking to family members and friends in the community. They thought that a lot of them were writing letters to the Board of Pardons and Paroles on my behalf. Looking into Julie's eyes, I could see the pain that she was dealing with, so I took her hand and said that I would be fine. I also said that I belonged to God and God said to me that I should not die. I knew that her faith was not completely with the Lord Jesus Christ, but I knew she believed in me. Tears began to roll down her face and she said, "I'm supposed to be here to help you, and it seems that I'm powerless to do anything."

I said, "That is not true. Your presence here plays a very important part in what is going on outside. When you leave, you will need to share with everyone that I said that I will be fine and will get out of this situation." With that said, the visitation door opened and my sisters entered the room. Regina had this strange look on her face that lead me to think she was wondering why I was with this white woman in the visiting room, in the South with an execution date only hours away. I told them that Julie was an attorney working for the legal defense fund, a branch of NAACP, and she had brought me up to speed on information.

I introduced my sisters to Julie and they thanked her for doing all she could to help me. Regina said, "The other day, I went to the Board of Pardons and Paroles to talk with some of the members, but they wouldn't see me individually. Their office was being flooded with William Moore's messages, letters, and people coming to the board." Regina did not tell anyone in the Board office that she was my sister. She just stood around and listened to the all of the workers in the offices complaining about having to handle the large volumes of mail and calls, and she felt good about what she saw. She asked me who all these people were and if I knew them all. I told her that over the years, I probably sent out letters to over a thousand folks, and this was people who know me; I was sure of that. Before going further with the visit, I suggested that we pray and thank the Lord for the day, because none of us would be here without Him. After the short prayer, I began to share with them what the Lord had revealed to me earlier that morning.

My sister, Norma Jean, said, "I know you will not die in the chair, and I guess my coming down here was to see if you knew and to help you see the light, because this knowing is a part of who you are and your heritage. Billy, it is a knowing within you. It is unexplainable, but you just know."

Yes, I did know, but how it would happen, I had no idea.

Many times, people would put on a front to hide how they are feeling in situations. Nevertheless, I have worked hard to stay in touch with my emotions, because all of the free thoughts pass through my mind if not controlled by comparing them to the word of God; knowing the choices I have to make and what God's Word said. If God said it, He will perform it and on time. By listening to God's Word, it brought peace and eased all fears. It is like being in a fight, and from out of nowhere comes your big brother to handle the situation; you can just sit back and watch it transpire.

Contemplating such thoughts transported me into a dream I had in 1981, only weeks before Judge Edenfield overturned my death sentence. I spoke to my visitors: "Let me tell you about a dream I had. It is as if I was standing outside of myself, watching things transpiring around me. There I was, sitting on the bed in the deathwatch cell; I had already been prepped for execution with my head and right leg already shaved. There was a spacey look on my face, as six big guards came inside the cell and everyone was watching me. The guards moved to grab me and stand me up, but the

47

warden said that I could walk without trouble. I stood up and faced the warden and said that I was ready, because the Lord just told me that I am not going to die. Walking out of the cell and over to the chair, I was helped by the guards to sit high on a pedestal so everyone could see me through the viewing glass. I saw many people in the audience, but not anyone's face I knew. The guards were busy putting the thick brown strap around my chest, legs, and forehead. The warden came in front of me and read the execution warrant and that the sentence was being carried out today. He asked me if I had any last words to say, and of course I apologized to the family of the victim and to all those who said I should die.

"A black cloth was put over my face. It seemed as if hours were passing by. I could hear my heart beating so hard that I thought I saw my shirt moving. There was total darkness and no sound. Then all of a sudden, it hit me. Hot currents like a liquid fire flowing from my head and up my leg and exploding at my heart. This was the worst pain I ever felt. It forced my body to push hard against the straps for what seemed like twenty minutes. As I watched myself being executed, I was terrified. It was horrendous, the worst thing I have ever seen. The doctor came over to me and checked for a heartbeat, and to everyone's surprise, I was still alive! The current had just passed through me without causing any harm. I could hear the doctor telling Warden Zant and Governor George Busbee that I was not dead. The warden asked if I was unconscious or half-dead. The doctor said 'It was as if he has not been executed at all.' The electric chair was checked and it was found to be in working order with all the proper connections. The governor said to do it again. Once again, the same thing happened. The doctor checked me and said 'He is still alive.'

"As they discussed this, the governor said he thought that there was an unwritten law that stated that if you execute a prisoner three times and not kill him, then he would have to be set free. The governor and warden said that they could not go from trying to execute me to complete freedom, so they decided to return me to the deathwatch cell until they could figure out the proper steps to follow in returning me to death row. Everyone was shocked and bewildered. As I watched myself being taken out of the chair, the officers seemed to be very upset, because this did not go the way they wanted. As the black cloth was removed from my face, I saw the expression of peace on my face. It was the same inner peace that I was feeling right now. Never before had I felt this great connection of peace when I would recall this dream as it was today, and that lets me know that everything has its time and place."

My thoughts were interrupted by Julie saying that she was going to call the office in Atlanta to find out if there had been any news from Savannah since Judge Edenfield took the case last night. When she returned, she said that there was not any word from the courts, and to attorneys, that was good news. The attorneys felt that it was a sign that he might be the one to grant a stay of execution, since he was the judge who said that I should not have been given the death sentence in the first place.

The rest of the visit consisted of other friends and family stopping by and visiting in short intervals. Everyone was concerned about how Little Billy was doing. I had called Evelyn, my mother-in-law, to see how he was doing. She told me that it was bad for him in school because the other children were taunting him about his father on death row who was going to be executed; reporters were following him, wanting to talk to him. Of course, he was afraid and worried about his father. That was too much for a thirteen-year-old to handle. Ed Loring was willing to fly my son here to visit, but I felt that it would be too much for him. During these visitations, no one really wanted to talk about the pending date. I knew they did not talk about this because they felt that it might upset me and make these last hours unpleasant.

Chapter Four: God's Encouragement

My best friend, Warren McCleskey, who I had not seen since the first day of deathwatch, entered the same visitation room. Warren was someone I knew who really cared and understood how it was to be there on the row. We hugged and started talking between ourselves, as our visitors were left to talk with each other. Once the officers saw us talking to each other and not with our visitors, he told me that I was not here to visit with McCleskey, and we needed to stop and move back to our families or he would cancel the visit altogether. Warren and I continued to talk about the processes that I had to go through and what was still ahead. It was like a revelation to my family, because they had not asked me what I did or had to do on the trip to the deathwatch cell. They had not asked how it was or asked about the chair.

Warren told me that some of the Christian brothers and others had taken it upon themselves to fast and pray for me, which was special. I began to tell Warren about the revelation that the Lord had given me earlier. I told him to tell the inmates not to worry, and that I would be all right and would be back to continue our Bible study groups. He asked me if I was afraid, and what deathwatch was like. I shared with him about the real hard struggle I had in gaining control of my thoughts at first. How they were running rampant in my mind. As you know, the control over my life is the Lord's because I belong to Him, and whatever He wills for me, that is what I'll gladly accept. Paul said *to live is gain, and to die he would immediately be in the presence of the Lord, which is blessed.* However, it was apparent to me that I would be around to continue teaching our Bible classes. "So tell the brothers to do the Bible readings and I will be there to finish our lesson. About fear, there is not any fear about the deathwatch process or the cell now, but in the beginning, that was the greatest battle. It is the same kind of cell, but a little bigger. The situation is much different, though; everything is focused on me directly. The State of Georgia is working tirelessly to kill me and making sure that nothing goes wrong with this execution. They wanted it nice, clean, and quiet, outside out of the public's view." I said, "If there is one thing that I have learned over these few hours, it is **that it's not where we are physically, but where we are in Christ that matters**. He is the center of my life and that is all what really counts. Coming to this point, I have found peace, comfort, and strength to keep me going in the midst of this situation."

The door of the visitation room opened and it was Carol and Denny McCrery with their children Lantz, Heidi, and Molly. I was completely surprised, because

I had only seen them twice since we'd known each other, and they were not on my visitation list. When I had asked to have them approved, it was denied. I wondered how in the world they got in the prison. I had no idea they would just drop everything abruptly, disrupt their schedules, pull their children out of school, and come south from Monmouth, Illinois to visit me. There was some large event going on in Atlanta, and all the rental car companies were out of cars, so they had to rent a limo from the Sunshine Limo Services just to come to the prison. What a sacrifice! This was another display of God's grace upon me and everyone involved in my life. They were beautiful people and full of the Holy Spirit.

I remember the way we met, about two years ago. I received a letter during the mail call with an address that I did not know. As I read the letter, the writer explained to me who they were and why they were writing. They had seen my name in a Christian magazine and they wrote to encourage me. This relationship between us took off from the very start, progressing into me being one of the family. We hugged each other and I introduced them to my sisters and to Warren, Ed, and Julie.

Denny spoke: "You know God has placed you in our lives and little did we know that we were not just writing this poor inmate on death row. We thought we were doing our Christian duty by ministering to you, but yet your letters were full of God's Word and you encouraged us. God knitted our hearts together as one. We called the warden and he told us that we could not see you, and do not come to the prison. We prayed and

53

sought the Lord about visiting you, and He told us to go anyway, and we would not have any problems getting in to see you."

Carol wanted to know all that had transpired since the last exchange of letters. Once again, I rehashed all that had happened. I told them about how I was going to live and not die in the electric chair, and how we are to stand steadfast in the Lord, believing that this is already done. "Therefore, don't be sad about tomorrow thinking that I will be executed. Know that I shall not die, but live just as the Lord has said." Denny asked me what was the work that I was to do. I said, "Just like the Lord said, to declare His works. Would you believe it? Here I am sitting on deathwatch, and before you know it, I'll be back on death row, teaching the other men about the mighty works of God that is displayed through His grace. Everyone will have to take notice and say that there is a God in heaven that hears the cries of those who truly love and give themselves to Him. It really does pay to serve the Lord Jesus Christ in this lifetime. I believe that anyone who does not have a personal relationship with the Lord already has a death sentence, and they are on death row of the world, and each person will need to receive God's special commutation to a sentence of eternal life."

Everyone in the visiting room wanted to know what I knew about my case, because it had been my custom to be on top of every decision made concerning my case as I kept abreast of the news from my attorneys and the courts. However, I had purposed in my heart not to watch the television, listen to the radio, or read the newspapers, so that I would not become distracted and lose my focus on what God was saying to me. So honestly, I did not know what was going on in the case, other than what Julie had told me. Julie came back from making her call and she said that Judge Edenfield had not made any ruling at that time. The officer informed me that I had five minutes left to visit. With that, we all started saying our good-byes and stood forming a circle as each one of us prayed. Then, turning towards Warren, I said again, "Tell the brothers that I will be back tomorrow."

Carol and Denny told me to write them after all of this was over, when they got home, to tell them every detail of what happened. I told my sisters that I would see them tomorrow, and told Julie to be encouraged, and watch God work things out. Ed gave me one of his bear hugs and said that he loved me, then the officers made everyone leave the visiting room.

Once again, I was taken to the small bathroom, where I had to strip naked in front of the officers; I wondered how the officers felt about looking at another man naked all the time. When I was in the army and worked as guard in the stockades, I never like conducting strip searches of other soldiers. It was humiliating for both of us. Back in my death cell, the officers would not take off the handcuff or leg irons, claiming that they didn't have orders to do so. It seems mighty strange to me that I could be in the visiting room with my family without chains on and no one said a word about that, and then the deathwatch cell, having to wear them did not make any sense at all.

I asked the officer who was operating the telephone to call the assistant warden and ask him what the procedures were. After he got off the phone, he told the other officer to remove the chains.

Four letters were on the bed, and as I read them, I had to fight back the tears because they were so brokenhearted, thinking that God was not going to deliver me from the execution. I tried to understand and think how they might be thinking about this situation, putting myself in their shoes so that I could write and comfort them. It came to my mind how each relationship started as pen pals, and from there it grew to family members over the years. We went through many things together and how God delivered us through them all. They had become involved in my case, watching the court system and believing that we would win a victory somewhere along the line, but this to them was a great defeat, and where was our God now?

After trying to feel all of their possible emotions, I prayed and felt that I was ready to answer their letters, because I now understood how they felt, and believed that God had given me the Word for them to overcome just as I had. He had give me the Word and I overcame in the face of defeat. I began to write them according to the Word that the Lord had given me, which was "…I shall not die, but live and declare the works of the Lord. The Lord has chastened me sore, but He hath not given me over unto death." Writing always gave me so much joy, knowing that it was ministering to my friends, because writing always allowed me to decrease as the power of the Holy Spirit Lord came forth and ministered to each person's needs; God flowed freely into the lives of my friends, and that was awesome!

Many people were looking forward to my execution. The crowds were gathering outside of the prison, waiting for this sideshow to take place. It became so bad that the prison had to set some boundaries around the prison to keep the people away. However, I was in the midst of peace in my mind; it was just one more day before God would do something so great that the legal world would have to take notice. I couldn't sleep because I was trying to guess how God was going to do it, so I lay on the bed and started this relaxation exercise that I learned about seven years ago. This technique taught me how to relax my whole body by tightening each muscle, then slowly loosening each one at a time, to gain control over every muscle in my body. However, while doing this process of relaxing, I would spend hours just lying on the bed in a semi-conscious state. This slowed my heart rate and breathing down. This was so comfortable and refreshing, it was as if I had been asleep for six hours.

Then I got up and began to pray for my friends and their families. Many wrote letters to the Board of Pardons and Paroles, because they felt that they had to do something physically for me. But when they asked me if I thought it was good for them to write letters on my behalf, my response was that it was solely their choice, and they should do what they believed God was leading them to do. I always say, we need to remember that once the letters, motions, and petitions are filed and the issues are argued, that was all we could do. Then we would have to trust in the Lord who has the power to change the minds of those in power. (The Bible says that the heart of the king is in God's hands, and He will turn him like the course of a river.) God is the only one that can change people's minds and opinions about me.

This sort of trust was a very hard lesson for me to learn, because at one point in my appeal process, I was my own attorney on the case until the Lord blessed me with what I believe are the best attorneys in the country. Nevertheless, I still was very involved in my case to the point where I had my attorneys send me rough draft copies of every petition and motion before it was filed in the courts. I would make changes, add new law issues, and I found myself fighting against what God was doing in me. He was teaching me how to completely trust in Him, because it was time for me to stop working and start completely trusting.

I surely believed God was going to bring it to pass. I didn't care if anyone believed or not; I did, and that was all that mattered to me. My mind tried to figure it out. God will bring the stay of execution from the Southern District Court, or the Eleventh Circuit Court of Appeals, or the United States Supreme Court, and naturally none of these looked promising. With each thought, I would dismiss it and say "Lord, it's in your hands."

I was excited because this was my last day on deathwatch, and the stay would be forthcoming, so I started singing, "This is the day that the Lord has made especially for me and I will be glad and rejoice in it." I told the officers that it had been nice, but these accommodations on deathwatch left a lot to be desired, and I would be leaving them today. I thought that this day was like one of them in the Old Testament where

God showed His power; now I was going to experience it firsthand. All of the doubters who thought that they would not see my face anymore would truly be amazed at the power of God. This was just like the Lord to wait until everything looked hopeless and then step in and stop it. I was so excited that I had to do some exercise to burn off some of the energy; I did not want to walk back and forth in my cell, because I surely did not want them to think I was afraid.

The head cook showed up with the breakfast and I told him that I wasn't eating, and that I didn't want a last meal either, because I would not be here to eat it. He just ignored me and left the food tray in the cell door and walked away, shaking his head. The lieutenant from death row came around the corner and asked me if there was anything I needed. I said, "This is my last day and I will be back on the row today, so keep my old cell open, and please do not let the office send my personal things out, because I will need them." He asked me if I had gotten any good news from the courts. I said, "The only good news that I have received was from the Lord, and I'll get a stay today. Just watch and see it come to pass, and know that I told you first this morning."

I requested permission to take a shower. The officer got on the phone and called somebody to see if it was all right if I could be out of my cell for any reason. Whomever he spoke to said that it was okay, but he had to wait for extra security, since this was the day of execution. The extra security was unnecessary, yet I understood. Within a few minutes, three huge officers appeared in full riot gear. They positioned themselves around the cell door. I was told to walk to the shower naked. Now I was wondering if all of this was worth a shower, when I could have washed up in the sink as I did the day before. As I moved towards the shower, so did the half-circle of officers, and they watched me take a shower. The funny part about all of this was the fact that the shower was very small and open, so all the water easily splashed out into the area where the officers where standing. Of course they all got soaked, and I did not help any by turning around and around, causing more water to splash on them. I had to laugh because it was so funny. I finished my shower and returned to my cell, dried off, and waited for my visitors.

Chapter Five:
The Third Day

I looked at the three riot guards, wondering if these guys would be with me all day. When the time came for me to go to the visiting room, I had to endure a strip search from the officers. As I handed them my clothes through the cell bars, I thought that they were going to tear them apart looking through the seams and every square inch of the material, before they passed them back. And of course, I had to turn around and let them look at my behind and spread the cheeks. I was so glad that this was the last day, because this was getting so crazy! It made me want to scream sometimes, "What you are looking for?! You have been watching me for the last two days and you know that I do not have anything, so what is all of this for?!"

But I keep my cool, and said that it's just about over and I want to see my family, and it's the price that I have to pay, being a death row inmate, moreover one on deathwatch..

I wondered about Mom and Dad Guthrie; would they show up today? That started me remembering how we first met when I was in the county jail. My first execution date was September 13, which was a Friday, and at that point in my life, I did not know anything about God or the Lord Jesus Christ. Around the first of the month, my cousin—whom I only knew as Aunt Peggy—wrote me a letter asking me if I wanted to be saved, and did I know the Lord? I wrote her back, telling her that I had a death sentence and at this time in my life, I thought that it was too late to be telling me anything about God. She was a member of Brittenal Apostolic Church in Columbus, Ohio under the leadership of Elder Hardy. She told her pastor that I had a death sentence and was to be executed shortly and that I needed to know Christ before I died; could he help? Elder Hardy called Elder and Mother Guthrie of Rome, Georgia, told them the story, and asked them if they could go to the county jail and see me. On September 6, early Saturday morning, they drove 250 miles one way on a very rainy day to come and see a man that they had never seen, just to tell him about Jesus. No one told me that they were coming to visit me, and at that point in my jail life, I really didn't care if I lived or died.

The shocker was that around noontime, the sheriff himself (Zollie Compton) came upstairs to the jail cell and said, "Moore, there is a preacher downstairs that wants to see you."

I said, "I didn't sent for any preacher and I ain't going downstairs to see one."

The sheriff looked at me as if I was crazy and said, "Boy! This is my jail and don't you ever forget that! Who in the hell do you think that you are telling me what you are not going to do! You better get your ass up and come on out of that cell or else!"

Since I knew that he was upset by what I said, and the fact that he was six-foot-five and over 300 pounds, I wasn't about to make another mistake like that, so when the door opened, I walked out with a smile on my face and said "Yes sir, let's go."

In the sheriff's office sat a man and woman. The man got up, extended his hand, and said, "Son, I'm Elder Guthrie and this is my wife Evangelist Guthrie. Your aunt Peggy of Columbus, Ohio contacted us, and her pastor also told us about your execution date for this Friday the thirteenth, and that you do not know the Lord Jesus Christ. Being moved with compassion, we are here today to share with you these things: We understand that you killed a man, but there is a just judge in heaven and his name is Jesus, and God LOVES you, he died for you! Jesus loves you just as you are and wants you to come to him with all of your guilt and sin and He will grant you peace that surpasses anything you have ever known. This love will overflow in your life. For the Bible says for you to repent and be baptized in the name of Jesus Christ for the remission of your sins and you shall receive the gift of the Holy Spirit. Son, don't you want to give your life to the Lord?"

In my mind, I could hear my thoughts saying, *I do not know who in the world these people are and I don't want to hear about this Jesus mess.* In my mind, it was too late to be talking God stuff; my execution date was only six days away. But as I looked into their eyes and saw their compassion, feeling the power of the Holy Spirit flowing from them, touching my heart and feeling the power of love from them, I knew in my heart what they were telling me was right and this was my last chance, for once in my life to do something right. When Elder Guthrie asked me if I wanted to accept the Lord into my life, inwardly my heart was shouting YES!

But I said, "What do I need to do to accept the Lord?"

Mom Guthrie said, "You need to repent by asking God to forgive you of all your sins and turn away from that sort of life. Confess to the Lord by telling Him that you are godly sorry, and believe that Jesus Christ died on the cross just for you, to forgive you of all your sins and that He rose from the dead so that you would be justified and have everlasting life. And then be baptized in the name of Jesus, and as Peter said, you shall receive the gift of the Holy Spirit with the evidence of speaking in other tongues like the people in the book of Acts did." After that, they took me through repentance and confessing my sins. Mom Guthrie said to the sheriff that they had to baptize me right now. He said that there was no way I was leaving the jail. However, there was a small bathtub on the porch that they could use if they wanted.

So we moved out to the porch and they started filling the little tub with water and started singing: "Take me to the water to be baptized, in the name of Jesus." One thing I know for sure is that my whole life had changed on that porch when I gave my life to the Lord. Elder Guthrie asked me to get in the water on my knees and he would take me under the water backwards, I told him that I could not do that, because my right knee had been operated on and it would not bend that far backwards. With that, Mom Guthrie said, "Sit the boy in the tub and let his legs hang over the edge, then take him backward from a sitting position and baptize the top half of him and then drag his legs through the water and baptize the bottom half of him, that should do it."

Coming up out of that water, I have never felt so clean and free in a moment's time and with a changed life. I knew that God was now a very important part of whatever life I had left, and I was truly happy. Later on, I did receive the baptism of the Holy Spirit with the evidence of speaking in other tongues, just like in the Bible.

My thoughts were interrupted by the officer telling me that I needed to turn around and let them put the chains on so that we could start for the visiting room. As we entered the room, I saw everyone: Norma Jean, Regina, Julie, Ed, and Murphy Davis his wife; she had been working on my case, talking to people in the wrens and family members of Mr. Stapleton. I guess that since this was my last day, she wanted to spend some time with me; we go back to 1978. She is a beautiful woman who has a real heart for death row inmates. I remember when their daughter Hannah was born, they brought her to Reidsville State Prison and gave me the opportunity to hold this new life. I hadn't held a baby in a long time; I was sort of scared to do so, but she encouraged me and that was a special joy for me. Here I was, a death row inmate, holding new life in my arms! There wasn't another person in the country who had worked so hard for us guys on death row. The newspapers started calling her the Angel of Death Row, because she just kept going. No matter how many roadblocks the state would throw in her way, God would give her the grace to get around them all and accomplish the goal.

Julie started with the first report that Judge Edenfield still had the case, and that in itself had everyone wondering if that was a good thing or bad, especially since he was taking up all the time. But he was the first judge to overturn my death sentence, saying that I should have never gotten the sentence in the first place. But the Eleventh Circuit reversed him two years ago. After some small talk, we all prayed, but my thoughts were settled and I was not in a state of denial. I just would not let my mind believe anything other than what the Lord had told me.

My main concern was what my friends and family were going through at this time. One of the greatest tests that we all had to face was at 10:30, when the word came that Judge Edenfield had just denied the motion to stop the execution. I really was not surprised, but this was a tug on my heart, seeing the reaction of my family and the others. I said, "We still have the Eleventh Circuit Court of Appeals, so do not worry. It shall be all right and besides all of that, it is in God's hands."

I am not sure who called the resource center and talked with my attorneys, but they said that we had drawn the worst three-judge panel on the Court, and it looked bad. After a short silence, I looked at everyone to make sure they were all right, and then continued with the visit, trying to enjoy the time that we had. Personally, I had to dig down deep within myself and grab hold of God's promise to me, and push away any negative thought out of my mind. Near the end of the visit, word came that the Eleventh Circuit had denied the motion to stop the execution. That news put everyone on edge, as things were moving to the United States Supreme Court, and their record was less than desirable when it came to death penalty cases and stopping executions. Therefore, many in the group said that their hope was not in the Supreme Court, but in the Board of Pardons and Paroles.

The assistant warden came and cut the visit short, saying that it was time for me to be back in the deathwatch cell so that I could be prepared for execution. This set of good-byes was the hardest because it seemed like everyone was acting as if this was the last time they would see me alive. My sisters did great; they didn't cry or fall apart. We hugged and kissed and everyone was made to leave.

After everyone had gone, it was just the officers and me. However, I felt a great peace about the whole situation as we walked over to the room to go through the strip search. The three riot guards were gone and it was as if the spirit of death that was over the prison had lifted. Everything was so different; even the officers didn't have that serious look on their faces that they had for the last two days. And yet, they didn't say anything to me, other than telling me to hand them parts of my clothing. All of this was out of character and just plain weird. The officers seemed to have some distant look on their faces, like they were in deep thought about something. I got dressed and all of the leg irons and handcuffs were put on—this time very loosely which even caused me to wonder if these guys were feeling sorry for me before they took me back to the deathwatch cell.

My thoughts wandered back to the time when I was going to be sentenced in 1974. One of the sheriff's deputies took off the leg irons and the handcuffs on the way to the courthouse and said, "Moore, you can run if you want to, so that I can shoot you. I'm the best shot on the force. Go ahead and try your luck."

One of the officers shocked me when he asked the other officers, "Do you want to take Moore by death row so that he can see it for the last time?" Then they both turned to me and said, "Do you want to go by there before we take you back to the deathwatch cell?"

I said, "Of course. I'm not in any hurry to get back to the deathwatch cell anyhow."

With that, we started walking around the prison the long way, and as we passed other inmates in the hallway, neither of the officers said a word to them or made them face the wall.

I was truly baffled by the officers' actions and I just couldn't put my finger on what was going on. I was not about to make any waves or say anything to them. As we walked down the hallway, passing the officers' mess hall, I didn't see the riot guards in there either. That was the place where they stayed most of the time when an execution was scheduled. Maybe they had gone to their stations around the prison and were in the death watch area and I would see all of them once we got in that area. So I just dismissed the idea of them being gone from the prison altogether.

We turned left, heading down a long hallway that seemed like it took us forever to reach the end. We passed the inmate store and continued on towards death row. I felt like I didn't have an execution date in just a little over seven and a half hours. Everything seemed like I was just returning from a regular visit.

The spirit of death that had been hanging over the whole prison was broken. There are principalities, major evil spirits that are placed over cities and people, to bring about the destruction of lives. I am sure that my life was one of those which Satan wanted to destroy, but God said that "I shall not die, but live and declare the works of the Lord!" As we got closer to the death row cell house, things appeared to get lighter and I saw more inmates out, just walking in the halls and in the other cellblocks. When we came to the gate of F-house, they were already open and the officers were on the other end of the cellblock, talking to an inmate, not paying any attention to us walking through the cellblock.

Entering the death row area where the counselor's and captain's office were, we saw nobody in any of these offices. We were walking towards the gate that led into the death row cellblock when one of the officers said, "Okay, we have seen enough, and we better get you back to deathwatch cell before they start looking for us." As we turned around to leave, Big Sergeant Johnny Cash appeared, as if he came form nowhere, and said to the officers, "Where are you taking Moore?"

They replied, "To deathwatch." With that, both of the officers looked at each other with a stare, as if they were saying to each other, *We are caught and in some big trouble.* I thought that they were in serious trouble for bringing me over to death row. Sergeant Cash said, "Why do you still have those chains on him?" Then all three of us looked at each other with stupid looks on our faces. Did he know what was going on or did he just get here today and not know about the execution tonight?

While we stood there speechless, before anyone could say a word, Sergeant Cash's thunderous voice said, "TAKE THOSE CHAINS OFF OF MOORE RIGHT NOW! DON'T YOU KNOW THAT HE HAS GOTTEN A STAY OF EXECUTION?"

I said, "A what? When? Who gave it to me?" It was like fireworks on the Fourth of July, all the excitement exploding in my mind. I shouted, "Thank you <u>Jesssus!</u> Lord, you said that I would not die!" Then I turned to the officers and said, "Didn't I tell you that it would happen!" YES…God is good and greatly to be praised! I was on cloud ninety-nine. All of the things that I had felt and seen in the hallways began to make sense to me about what was happening on the way to death row.

I asked the officers, didn't they know about the stay, and was that the reason why they brought me by death row? They said that they had no idea, and it was a surprise to them too.

Sergeant Cash said, "The Eleventh Circuit Court of Appeals just issued you an indefinite stay of execution." With a big smile on his face, he was a giant of a man, about six-foot-four and 300-plus pounds, then he told me to come into the office, and said to the officers, "You two go over to the deathwatch cell and bring anything that Moore had left in the cell, because he will be going back on death row immediately." Looking at me and shaking his head, he said, "You mean to tell me that you knew nothing about the stay?"

I said, "When my visit was ended around 5:00, it was said to me and my family by the assistant warden that the Eleventh Circuit had just denied my case, and the next step would be the U.S. Supreme Court, and for the officers to bring me on my way to be prepared for execution."

He replied, "A lot can happen in fifteen minutes, huh?"

Cash said, "Well, Moore, all of your belongings are still here in the buggy in the captain's office. Of course, you know that you have to give those new clothes back you are wearing, and the shoes, put on your old things, and no one has moved into your old cell. As a matter of fact, it's open for you right now."

It was indeed a miracle, and just like the Lord said, I would not die, but live and declare the works of the Lord. After changing into my old clothes, taking the buggy and rolling it into the cellblock, I screamed, "I am back!" and pandemonium broke out everywhere! All the inmates just went crazy, banging their cups on the bars, shouting "Moor-Man, it's good to see you again! I knew that you were going to get a stay!" "They lost this time!" "Come over here and shake my hand, man, is that really you!"

You would've thought that everybody on the row had gotten their death sentence commuted by all the mass excitement in the cellblock.

It was a grand feeling to be home, but most of all to know that God's word is true, and others will see the faithfulness of the Lord. This miracle should turn some more hearts around in this cellblock. Tears of joy flowing down my face cannot even begin to express the wave after wave of happiness and peace washing over me. It was as if I was a different person, and all of us were elevated above our surroundings of being on death row, the goodness of God that was all over me. I shall forever stand on the word that God gave me; I shall not die, but live and declare the works of the Lord!

Chapter Six:
The Arrest

Things were moving so fast, I do not recall carrying the buggy up the steps to my cell. Guys were calling me—"Come over here and let me touch, or let me see your face." The next thing I realized was that I was sitting down on my bed, feeling completely exhausted, like a million tons had just been lifted off my shoulders. I was unable to focus, as my thoughts were being drowned by the loud noise of the inmates in the cellblock, shouting, screaming, calling out my name… "Moor-man, how does it feel to be back?" "I told you that those bloodsuckers weren't going to win this time." "You should have seen the look on the guards' faces when they found out that you got a stay and that they would not be able to kill you."

In the midst of all the voices, I heard the familiar sound of the cell doors opening as the shift of inmates was let out of their cells to complete their three hours of out-of-cell time; the sound of feet running, hitting the steps. As I turned towards the bars, there was

Charlie Corn standing there with a big smile on his face. He said, "Man, it is sure good to see you again. It has been a rough three days for me and I was a nervous wreck. Tell me what was it like being on deathwatch. Were the guards mean? What did you order for your last meal?"

I said, " Hold on with all of the questions. We now have time to go through everything you want to know, but right now I just want to sit here and appreciate being alive."

I listened to Charlie, watched him shake my cell door, rattling it back and forth while he was screaming "It's good to see you, man!" over and over…in his excitement! The cell house officer's voice came over the intercom, saying, "Count time, everybody locks up!" Charlie said, "I'll see you in the morning when your shift comes out."

The cell doors slammed shut, and at the same time I heard the keys for the hallway gate, then the electric gates slammed closed as the officers started up the steps. Usually, one of the officers would count the inmates downstairs and the other would count the upstairs, but both officers came upstairs. These were two officers that I didn't know and had never seen. As they came to my cell, one of them looked at me with eyes full of hatred and said, "Moore, we'll get your ass the next time, and you won't be so lucky then."

I could not contain myself from laughing and saying, "Praise God, this is the work of the Lord and there is nothing you can do about it, because God said that I shall not die, but live, and declare the works of the Lord!" I knew there were many officers who believed in the death penalty and had volunteered to be on the doom squads to handle the executions. They were the strap down team, who placed the inmate in the electric chair and strapped him down. Even those who would push one of the three buttons, which would send the electric chair into action and bring about the electrocution of the inmates. I had not met any officer who took the executions as personally as this officer did. I thought to myself that I wasn't going allow what anyone said to me steal my joy of the miracle God had just performed for me in the sight of the world.

I knew that for the next three hours, when this last shift would come out of their cells for the night, I would not get any rest. Because up to this point in our lives on death row, no one had ever gone to deathwatch and come within seven hours of execution and then received a stay of execution. This was unheard of, and what made this so extraordinary was the fact that I was guilty and everybody knew it! That's what made the grace of God so amazing and special. Even the non-believers had to agree that this was a miracle!

As soon as the cell doors for the third shift were open, there were many inmates in front of my cell saying "Let me touch you or shake your hand to see if you are alive." All of this seemed so unreal, but with the excitement and joy that I felt, I could understand and feel their joy and happiness too, because this just was not a victory for me, but for all death-row inmates. Because if I could get a stay of execution, being that close to death, then there was hope for everyone on death row! No matter how close to death anyone would come, I would be a symbol of hope.

As I stood up and walked towards the bars to shake hands with my fellow inmates, listening to what they were saying, suddenly my mind transported me back to April 4, 1974, where I saw myself sitting in an army classroom at Fort Gordon, Georgia, working on a signal generator. I saw a black probe from a voltage meter in my right hand and a vacant expression on my face. As I was searching for the correct spot to check the voltage, POW!!! An explosion... I had touched the wrong terminal; I felt the sparks fly into my face, causing a stinging pain. But the pain that was etched into my face had nothing to do with the sparks from the explosion. My head was hung low, my eyes were filled with tears, and I could not see what I was supposed to be doing, because I was slowly dying as my mind, my soul, and my spirit were screaming at me. The reality of last night began to piece itself together... the frightful truth is what really exploded in my mind!

I saw on the screen of my mind, my thoughts creating a picture showing me that I had shot and killed a man... the voice of others' thoughts saying *maybe he wasn't dead...* I don't know... I don't clearly remember... I began to see small glimpse of truth surfacing and terrorizing my mind because it was true and unbelievable. Yet, in my heart I knew that he was dead and it was tearing me apart... killing me... I had destroyed the lives of many people... Broken others' hearts... I had no peace... My soul was in turmoil... How in the world could I ever live with myself... I was under a tremendous burden... What am I going to do... What shall I do?

The struggle continued in my mind. I was saying to myself that I must turn myself in to the police. *But I can't, because I have my son, Billy living with me…* These thoughts screamed in my mind… *Your son? You just killed someone else's son, brother, and father… You must turn yourself in to the police!*

I could not abandon him like my father did to me when he went to prison when I was four years old. I never wanted Billy to go through that same pain, that shame, that suffering I went through all of my life; and yet I had destroyed his young life too.

I saw my head drop into my hands as the pain ran back and forth through my heart just like alternating current. I was saying why… why… why…. why… did I listen to George, let him fill my head with all that crazy mess?

"Come on, Moore, this will be easy and no one will get hurt because no one will be home. We can just go into the house and get the money because I know where it is and that will handle all of your problems. Come on, Moore, let's smoke this joint and everything will be all right. This will calm your nerves. Here, have some Jack Daniel's with me." Before long, the whole fifth was gone! "How about a cold beer, one to wash that bad taste out of your mouth?" Two beers… three beers… who was counting anymore?

Once the drugs and alcohol reached their greatest effect on the both of us, we were beyond what one would call being drunk or high; we were out of our minds. George said, "Follow me," as we staggered out of his front door into the dark of the night. We crossed a street, and from that point, I was lost and had no idea where we were, or where we were going. I just stayed behind him, holding onto his shirt until we came to a back porch. He said that the door was open and I followed him into the house. I do not know if it was my inebriated condition or the room we entered was just that dark, but I could not see a thing, not even my own hand in front of my face.

I felt myself being pulled next to a door that George said was locked from the inside, and we should ram it with our shoulders. We did, but the door would not give, even after about three or four times of hurting our shoulders and falling on the floor after each time we hit the door. In the midst of all the noise we must've made, somewhere in all that madness, we returned to George's house, where we resumed our drinking— wine this time—and smoking more pot for the next few hours. I remember telling George that I had to go home because I had to report to school at Fort Gordon in the morning. Somehow, I got in my car and drove off into the darkness.

The scene in my mind shifted, and the next picture I saw was my hand turning the door handle of my trailer door to open it because someone had knocked on it. Immediately I saw myself flying through the air outside of the trailer and being thrown to the ground. When I opened my eyes, all I saw was shotgun barrels and pistols pointed inches above my face. I saw all of my clothes being torn off my body. As I lay naked on the ground, the sheriff said, "You are under arrest for murder."

There were five officers from Jefferson County, ten from Richmond County, and four Georgia Bureau of Investigation (GBI) officers. I was rolled over, handcuffed, taken back into my trailer, and slammed down into a chair, as the officers searched through the whole trailer without finding anything.

Then the sheriff said, "We know that you committed this murder, so tell me where the money is. We have George outside in a car. He told us all about it and he brought us here to arrest you."

At that point, one of the officers came out of the back bedroom with Billy Jr. and said, "What shall we do with this child?" One of the GBI officers asked me if I knew of anyone I could leave him with, because tonight I was going to jail. I told him that two trailers down on the right was a friend of mine, and they could leave Billy with him until one of my sisters from Columbus, Ohio could come and get him. With that, the officer left the trailer with Billy. My worst fear had just come true; not wanting him to be without a father, now he was without either parent.

It was at that point a great peace had come over me. It was over and I could rest. I did not need to struggle within myself anymore. The police were there and I was glad. I said to the sheriff, "If you look in the heating duct, you will find the money in two envelopes, and the pistol, and I am very sorry that I caused all of this pain. I didn't mean to hurt anybody."

The sheriff said, "I am tried of you damn Yankees coming down here to my county and committing crimes. I ought to shoot you down like a dog right where you sit."

As he reached for his gun, one of the BGI officers said to him, "I will handle it from here, Zollie."

Zollie said to me, "I will see that you'll get the death sentence."

I was placed in the back seat of a police car between two BGI officers. I was taken to the Louisville City Police Station. As we were entering the station, I saw two ladies. I didn't know who they were, but I felt in my heart that they were relatives of the man I had killed. I stopped and said to them, "I am so sorry... I'm sorry... I'm sorry.... I didn't mean to...."

The GBI officers pulled me inside a room and sat me down in front of a tape recorder and said to me, "If you are so sorry, you will tell us everything that happened."

As I began to talk with the GBI officers, trying to remember what happened after I left George's house, words began to slowly tumble out of my mouth and it was like I was watching a video of myself. For the first time, I was hearing and seeing everything that happened that night, actually seeing it happening in my mind in slow motion. I felt sick and disgusted at what I was saying, as if I had died too. I lost all feeling and emotions, as the words poured forth like knives, cutting my own spirit in pieces as I listened to myself.

Leaving George's house with intentions of going home, I missed my turn and drove completely around the circle a few times. I found myself stopping in a Laundromat parking lot, because there was light and hopefully I could find some help in getting to Highway 1 heading south. Getting out of the car and looking into the Laundromat, I saw nobody and I started walking down the street. The street appeared to be deserted, at least that's what I thought, not seeing anyone nor knowing exactly where I was. I was thinking surely George's house had to be in this direction as I was walking.

Then... a strong inner urge hit me like a flashing neon light in a hotel window that said to me, "THIS IS THE HOUSE!" I knew that this was the house, because I heard it in my mind as if someone said aloud, *this is it;* I heard it. I saw myself turn and walk up the steps. (I had never seen this house before from the front street, other than our coming over here earlier that night. All I saw then was the back door, and I was too drunk to know how we got there and back to George's house.)

I went to the front door, knocked on the door, waited for someone to answer. When no one did, I tried the knob. It was locked. As I turned to leave, this inner voice said that the window was open. Going over to the window, I pushed it open and stepped through into a world of pitch darkness. I could not see a thing. I had no idea what room I was in, but I just turned to the right and walked around the walls until I came to another door that was locked.

Standing in front of the door, I start knocking on the door. Due to my stupidity and because of my intoxication, I was unaware of the door opening away from me into the room. Then a shotgun barrel hit me in the leg and exploded at the same time. Fear paralyzed my mind, and out of response, as I jumped, my hand grabbed the barrel. I pulled the pistol out of my pants and fired into the darkness. I stood there trembling and holding the shotgun barrel for what felt like hours.

I took a few steps forward, then a string hit me in the face. I pulled it, and a light came on. There was the man I shot, lying face down. I didn't see any blood on him or on the floor. I did not know if I had indeed shot him or not. I didn't hear anything. As I looked around the room, my thoughts were screaming at me, "What are you doing?"

I realized that George was the only one who knew where the money was. As I turned to leave, the thought was impressed on my mind to look under the pillow. Lifting the pillows, I saw two wallets. I took them and turned and walked to the front door, opened it and walked down the steps, down the middle of the street, still holding the shotgun in my left hand.

I made it to my car and opened the trunk, dropping everything in the trunk. Getting into the car is the last thing I remember. I don't know how I drove home; I just know that I was home. I put the money into two envelopes and wrote "G" on one for George. (I was really disgusted with myself to learn what happen that night as I told the GBI the whole story.)

After signing a statement saying that I gave this confession freely without any promises, I was taken to the Louisville County Jail, which looked like a regular house, but the jail was upstairs, and I was put in the first cell. THEN... all of this really hit me like an atomic bomb! I had really killed another human being. It didn't matter if I didn't mean to or not; I did it and I was responsible. My heart sank so low, I felt terrible and I began to hate myself. A great anger began to rise in my own mind that I should do something about it. I could hear the words in my mind saying *You must die. Your life isn't worth the air you breathe. How could you be so stupid, dumb, and crazy to take another man's life?!*

I lay there on the jailhouse bed crying and saying to myself, *What can I do? I have messed up all these people's lives, and not to say anything about my own family.* Getting off the bed, I called to the man in the cell next to me and asked him if he had a shaver that I could use, and he handed me one around the corner of the bars. I had purposed in my heart to kill myself that night in the county jail. In my grief and sorrow, I had broken open the single-edge razor and taken out the blade. I proceed to cut a sheet from the bed into six thin sections. I braided them into two long ropes, tied my legs down at the end of the bed with one, and used the other rope to tie across my chest. I pulled the wool blanket on top of me to hide the ropes, so if any of the guards came by the cell, all they could see from their angle would be me asleep in the bed.

I had already taken the washcloth and soaked it with soap and laid it at the head of the bed. Lathering soap onto the left side of my neck, I had every intention of cutting my throat and dying in that cell. With the blade in my hand and on my throat, ready to kill myself and put an end to all of this pain, I heard this booming, authoritative voice so clearly that it seized every thought in my mind and froze me physically in the act of cutting my throat. I do not know if it anyone else heard it, but it was real, and it had my attention.

I looked around and did not see anyone, which was enough for me to know that this was not my own thought. The voice said, "You are in pain, full of grief and condemnation. I heard you saying that you were sorry for committing this murder. Then why are you murdering again? Killing yourself will not relieve your pain, condemnation, guilt, and shame."

I said, "God, (for I knew that it could only be God speaking to me) I promise to you this night that I will never hurt another human being as long as I live." After that, I cut the ropes and sat up on the bed.

Warren McCleskey's voice singing, "God is a good God, yes…He is! Praise the Lord! Praise The Lord! Praise The Lord!!!" and his squeezing my hand snapped me out of the vision that I was seeing, back into reality. He pulled me closer to the bars and started slapping me on my shoulder in his excitement, saying, "Brother! We have never seen anything like this before, and you just watch how many of the non-believing inmates will come to the Lord. God has not saved you from the electric chair for nothing! Especially with you being guilty and not having any legal issues to stand on, this really shows the mercy of God, and everyone has to see it."

Epilogue

After being on death row for sixteen and a half years, Billy Neal Moore lost all of his appeals, faced with another execution date; the Georgia Board of Pardons and Parole reviewed his case. At the hearing, the members of the victim's family traveled over one hundred miles to the Paorle board in Atlanta and entered passionate pleaded for his life. Mother Theresa called from India, saying that the board should do what Jesus would do.

On August 21, 1990 just twenty hours prior to the execution the Board of Pardons and Paroles did what Jesus would do, they commuted his death sentence to a life sentence.

On November 8, 1991 the Board of Pardons and Paroles, with letters and petitions from victims' family released Billy Neal Moore from prison.

Since being released from prison he continuously speak in; prisons, juvenile detention centers, grade schools, high schools, Colleges and Universities, national conventions and churches all across America.

Ordain a minister in 1992 with the Pentecostal Assemblies of the World. Billy married Pastor Donna Jacks-Moore of Saganaw, Michigan, and they formed Christ Assembly Evaneglistic Ministries, teaching the love and Forgiveness of God. At 14 Wildwood Lane, NE. Rome, Georgia. 30161 Following the directions of the Lord the Moore's moved to Rome, Georgia in 1997 where they both assist Bishop Nealon Guthrie at Christ Temple Church. As they continue to travel around the country.

About the Author

Billy Neal Moore story is of a confessed, and convicted murderer who was sentenced to die in Georgia's electric chair in 1974. Overcome with remorse and grief for his crime, he wrote letters to members of the victim's family, apologizing for his crime.

They were so moved by his sincere sorrow, that they had compassion on him; forgiving him and continue to correspond with him for sixteen years. Being extremely grateful for their forgiveness, he not only turned his own life around, but he became determined to help transform the lives of everyone he touch with his salvaged soul.

Billy was forgiven for his heinous act by the members of the victim's family. After sixteen and a half years on death-row, teaching and preaching love and forgiveness which he received to his fellow inmates and to hundreds of folks around the country. His own life was spared seven hours prior to the execution.

At the impassion pleas of the victim's family and the unexpected intervention of Mother Theresa, Billy's death sentence was commuted by the Georgia Board of Pardons and parole to life.

Printed in the United States
29742LVS00002B/157-1008